'THE ALPHABET OF
THE TREES

IS FADING IN THE
SONG OF THE
LEAVES.'

WILLIAM CARLOS WILLIAMS
Born 1883, Rutherford, New Jersey, USA
Died 1963, Rutherford, New Jersey, USA

The poems in this selection are taken from *Al Que Quiere!*
(1917); *Sour Grapes* (1921); *Spring and All* (1923); *Collected Poems
1921–1931* (1934); *An Early Martyr* (1935); *The Complete Collected
Poems 1906–1938* (1938); *The Broken Span* (1941); *The Wedge* (1944);
The Clouds (1948); *The Collected Later Poems* (1950); and *Pictures
from Brueghel* (1962).

WILLIAMS IN PENGUIN MODERN CLASSICS
Selected Poems

WILLIAM CARLOS WILLIAMS

Death the Barber

PENGUIN BOOKS

PENGUIN CLASSICS

UK | USA | Canada | Ireland | Australia
India | New Zealand | South Africa

Penguin Books is part of the Penguin Random House group
of companies whose addresses can be found at
global.penguinrandomhouse.com.

This selection first published 2018
001

Copyright © William Carlos Williams, 1917, 1921, 1923, 1934, 1935, 1938,
1941, 1944, 1948, 1950, 1962

Set in 9.85/12.75 pt Dante MT Std
Typeset by Jouve (UK), Milton Keynes
Printed in Great Britain by Clays Ltd, St Ives plc

ISBN: 978–0–241–33982–4

www.greenpenguin.co.uk

Penguin Random House is committed to a
sustainable future for our business, our readers
and our planet. This book is made from Forest
Stewardship Council® certified paper.

Contents

Apology

Why do I write today?

The beauty of
the terrible faces
of our nonentities
stirs me to it:

colored women
day workers –
old and experienced –
returning home at dusk
in cast off clothing
faces like
old Florentine oak.

Also

the set pieces
of your faces stir me –
leading citizens –
but not
in the same way.

Pastoral

The little sparrows
hop ingenuously
about the pavement
quarreling
with sharp voices
over those things
that interest them.
But we who are wiser
shut ourselves in
on either hand
and no one knows
whether we think good
or evil.

      Meanwhile,
the old man who goes about
gathering dog-lime
walks in the gutter
without looking up
and his tread
is more majestic than
that of the Episcopal minister

approaching the pulpit
of a Sunday.
   These things
astonish me beyond words.

El Hombre

It's a strange courage
you give me ancient star:

Shine alone in the sunrise
toward which you lend no part!

Trees

Crooked, black tree
on your little grey-black hillock,
ridiculously raised one step toward
the infinite summits of the night:
even you the few grey stars
draw upward into a vague melody
of harsh threads.

Bent as you are from straining
against the bitter horizontals of
a north wind, – there below you
how easily the long yellow notes
of poplars flow upward in a descending
scale, each note secure in its own
posture – singularly woven.

All voices are blent willingly
against the heaving contra-bass
of the dark but you alone
warp yourself passionately to one side
in your eagerness.

Dedication for a Plot of Ground

This plot of ground
facing the waters of this inlet
is dedicated to the living presence of
Emily Dickinson Wellcome
who was born in England, married,
lost her husband and with
her five year old son
sailed for New York in a two-master,
was driven to the Azores;
ran adrift on Fire Island shoal,
met her second husband
in a Brooklyn boarding house,
went with him to Puerto Rico
bore three more children, lost
her second husband, lived hard
for eight years in St Thomas,
Puerto Rico, San Domingo, followed
the oldest son to New York,
lost her daughter, lost her 'baby',
seized the two boys of
the oldest son by the second marriage
mothered them – they being
motherless – fought for them
against the other grandmother

and the aunts, brought them here
summer after summer, defended
herself here against thieves,
storms, sun, fire,
against flies, against girls
that came smelling about, against
drought, against weeds, storm-tides,
neighbors, weasels that stole her chickens,
against the weakness of her own hands,
against the growing strength of
the boys, against wind, against
the stones, against trespassers,
against rents, against her own mind.

She grubbed this earth with her own hands,
domineered over this grass plot,
blackguarded her oldest son
into buying it, lived here fifteen years,
attained a final loneliness and –

If you can bring nothing to this place
but your carcass, keep out.

To Waken an Old Lady

Old age is
a flight of small
cheeping birds
skimming
bare trees
above a snow glaze.
Gaining and failing
they are buffeted
by a dark wind –
But what?
On harsh weedstalks
the flock has rested,
the snow
is covered with broken
seedhusks
and the wind tempered
by a shrill
piping of plenty.

Arrival

And yet one arrives somehow,
finds himself loosening the hooks of
her dress
in a strange bedroom –
feels the autumn
dropping its silk and linen leaves
about her ankles.
The tawdry veined body emerges
twisted upon itself
like a winter wind . . . !

The Eyeglasses

The universality of things
draws me toward the candy
with melon flowers that open

about the edge of refuse
proclaiming without accent
the quality of the farmer's

shoulders and his daughter's
accidental skin, so sweet
with clover and the small

yellow cinquefoil in the
parched places. It is
this that engages the favorable

distortion of eyeglasses
that see everything and remain
related to mathematics –

in the most practical frame of
brown celluloid made to
represent tortoiseshell –

A letter from the man who
wants to start a new magazine
made of linen

and he owns a typewriter –
July 1, 1922
All this is for eyeglasses

to discover. But
they lie there with the gold
earpieces folded down

tranquilly Titicaca –

The Right of Way

In passing with my mind
on nothing in the world

but the right of way
I enjoy on the road by

virtue of the law –
I saw

an elderly man who
smiled and looked away

to the north past a house –
a woman in blue

who was laughing and
leaning forward to look up

into the man's half
averted face

and a boy of eight who was
looking at the middle of

the man's belly
at a watchchain –

The supreme importance
of this nameless spectacle

sped me by them
without a word –

Why bother where I went?
for I went spinning on the

four wheels of my car
along the wet road until

I saw a girl with one leg
over the rail of a balcony

Death the Barber

Of death
the barber
the barber
talked to me

cutting my
life with
sleep to trim
my hair –

It's just
a moment
he said, we die
every night –

And of
the newest
ways to grow
hair on

bald death –
I told him
of the quartz
lamp

and of old men
with third
sets of teeth
to the cue

of an old man
who said
at the door –
Sunshine today!

for which
death shaves
him twice
a week

Young Sycamore

I must tell you
this young tree
whose round and firm trunk
between the wet

pavement and the gutter
(where water
is trickling) rises
bodily

into the air with
one undulant
thrust half its height –
and then

dividing and waning
sending out
young branches on
all sides –

hung with cocoons
it thins
till nothing is left of it
but two

eccentric knotted
twigs
bending forward
hornlike at the top

The Cod Head

Miscellaneous weed
strands, stems, debris –
firmament

to fishes –
where the yellow feet
of gulls dabble

oars whip
ships churn to bubbles –
at night wildly

agitate phosphores-
cent midges – but by day
flaccid

moons in whose
discs sometimes a red cross
lives – four

fathom – the bottom skids
a mottle of green
sands backward –

amorphous waver-
ing rocks – three fathom
the vitreous

body through which –
small scudding fish deep
down – and

now a lulling lift
and fall –
red stars – a severed cod –

head between two
green stones – lifting
falling

Poem

As the cat
climbed over
the top of

the jamcloset
first the right
forefoot

carefully
then the hind
stepped down

into the pit of
the empty
flowerpot

Nantucket

Flowers through the window
lavender and yellow

changed by white curtains –
Smell of cleanliness –

Sunshine of late afternoon –
On the glass tray

a glass pitcher, the tumbler
turned down, by which

a key is lying – And the
immaculate white bed

The Attic Which Is Desire

the unused tent
of

bare beams
beyond which

directly wait
the night

and day –
Here

from the street
by

```
  *   *   *
  *   S   *
  *   O   *
  *   D   *
  *   A   *
  *   *   *
```

ringed with
running lights

the darkened
pane

exactly
down the center

is
transfixed

This Is Just to Say

I have eaten
the plums
that were in
the icebox

and which
you were probably
saving
for breakfast

Forgive me
they were delicious
so sweet
and so cold

Death

He's dead
the dog won't have to
sleep on his potatoes
any more to keep them
from freezing

he's dead
the old bastard –
He's a bastard because

there's nothing
legitimate in him any
more
        he's dead
He's sick-dead

                he's
a godforsaken curio
without
any breath in it

He's nothing at all
        he's dead
shrunken up to skin

Put his head on
one chair and his
feet on another and
he'll lie there
like an acrobat –

Love's beaten. He
beat it. That's why
he's insufferable –

because
he's here needing a
shave and making love
an inside howl
of anguish and defeat –

He's come out of the man
and he's let
the man go –
                    the liar

Dead
        his eyes
rolled up out of
the light – a mockery
                              which
love cannot touch –

just bury it
and hide its face
for shame.

The Botticellian Trees

The alphabet of
the trees

is fading in the
song of the leaves

the crossing
bars of the thin

letters that spelled
winter

and the cold
have been illumined

with
pointed green

by the rain and sun –
The strict simple

principles of
straight branches

are being modified
by pinched-out

ifs of color, devout
conditions

the smiles of love –
. . . . . .

until the stript
sentences

move as a woman's
limbs under cloth

and praise from secrecy
quick with desire

love's ascendancy
in summer –

In summer the song
sings itself

above the muffled words –

Flowers by the Sea

When over the flowery, sharp pasture's
edge, unseen, the salt ocean

lifts its form – chicory and daisies
tied, released, seem hardly flowers alone

but color and the movement – or the shape
perhaps – of restlessness, whereas

the sea is circled and sways
peacefully upon its plantlike stem

Item

This, with a face
like a mashed blood orange
that suddenly

would get eyes
and look up and scream
War! War!

clutching her
thick, ragged coat
A piece of hat

broken shoes
War! War!
stumbling for dread

at the young men
who with their gun-butts
shove her

sprawling –
a note
at the foot of the page

View of a Lake

from a
highway below a face
of rock

too recently blasted
to be overgrown
with grass or fern:

Where a
waste of cinders
slopes down to

the railroad and
the lake
stand three children

beside the weed-grown
chassis
of a wrecked car

immobile in a line
facing the water
To the left a boy

in falling off
blue overalls
Next to him a girl

in a grimy frock
And another boy
They are intent

watching something
below – ?
A section sign: 50

on an iron post
planted
by a narrow concrete

service hut
(to which runs
a sheaf of wires)

in the universal
cinders beaten
into crossing paths

to form the front yard
of a frame house
at the right

that looks
to have been flayed
Opposite

remains a sycamore
in leaf
Intently fixed

the three
with straight backs
ignore

the stalled traffic
all eyes
toward the water

To a Poor Old Woman

munching a plum on
the street a paper bag
of them in her hand

They taste good to her
They taste good
to her. They taste
good to her

You can see it by
the way she gives herself
to the one half
sucked out in her hand

Comforted
a solace of ripe plums
seeming to fill the air
They taste good to her

The Yachts

contend in a sea which the land partly encloses
shielding them from the too-heavy blows
of an ungoverned ocean which when it chooses

tortures the biggest hulls, the best man knows
to pit against its beatings, and sinks them pitilessly.
Mothlike in mists, scintillant in the minute

brilliance of cloudless days, with broad bellying sails
they glide to the wind tossing green water
from their sharp prows while over them the crew crawls

ant-like, solicitously grooming them, releasing,
making fast as they turn, lean far over and having
caught the wind again, side by side, head for the mark.

In a well guarded arena of open water surrounded by
lesser and greater craft which, sycophant, lumbering
and flittering follow them, they appear youthful, rare

as the light of a happy eye, live with the grace
of all that in the mind is fleckless, free and
naturally to be desired. Now the sea which holds them

is moody, lapping their glossy sides, as if feeling
for some slightest flaw but fails completely.
Today no race. Then the wind comes again. The yachts

move, jockeying for a start, the signal is set and they
are off. Now the waves strike at them but they are too
well made, they slip through, though they take in
    canvas.

Arms with hands grasping seek to clutch at the prows.
Bodies thrown recklessly in the way are cut aside.
It is a sea of faces about them in agony, in despair

until the horror of the race dawns staggering the mind,
the whole sea become an entanglement of watery bodies
lost to the world bearing what they cannot hold. Broken,

beaten, desolate, reaching from the dead to be taken up
they cry out, failing, failing! their cries rising
in waves still as the skillful yachts pass over.

Autumn

A stand of people
by an open

grave underneath
the heavy leaves

celebrates
the cut and fill

for the new road
where

an old man
on his knees

reaps a basket-
ful of

matted grasses for
his goats

The Term

A rumpled sheet
of brown paper
about the length

and apparent bulk
of a man was
rolling with the

wind slowly over
and over in
the street as

a car drove down
upon it and
crushed it to

the ground. Unlike
a man it rose
again rolling

with the wind over
and over to be as
it was before.

The Poor

It's the anarchy of poverty
delights me, the old
yellow wooden house indented
among the new brick tenements

Or a cast-iron balcony
with panels showing oak branches
in full leaf. It fits
the dress of the children

reflecting every stage and
custom of necessity –
Chimneys, roofs, fences of
wood and metal in an unfenced

age and enclosing next to
nothing at all: the old man
in a sweater and soft black
hat who sweeps the sidewalk –

his own ten feet of it
in a wind that fitfully
turning his corner has
overwhelmed the entire city

These

are the desolate, dark weeks
when nature in its barrenness
equals the stupidity of man.

The year plunges into night
and the heart plunges
lower than night

to an empty, windswept place
without sun, stars or moon
but a peculiar light as of thought

that spins a dark fire –
whirling upon itself until,
in the cold, it kindles

to make a man aware of nothing
that he knows, not loneliness
itself – Not a ghost but

would be embraced – emptiness,
despair – (They
whine and whistle) among

the flashes and booms of war;
houses of whose rooms
the cold is greater than can be thought,

the people gone that we loved,
the beds lying empty, the couches
damp, the chairs unused –

Hide it away somewhere
out of the mind, let it get roots
and grow, unrelated to jealous

ears and eyes – for itself.
In this mine they come to dig – all.
Is this the counterfoil to sweetest

music? The source of poetry that
seeing the clock stopped, says,
The clock has stopped

that ticked yesterday so well?
and hears the sound of lakewater
splashing – that is now stone.

The Last Words of My English Grandmother

1920

There were some dirty plates
and a glass of milk
beside her on a small table
near the rank, disheveled bed –

Wrinkled and nearly blind
she lay and snored
rousing with anger in her tones
to cry for food,

Gimme something to eat –
They're starving me –
I'm all right I won't go
to the hospital. No, no, no

Give me something to eat
Let me take you
to the hospital, I said
and after you are well

you can do as you please.
She smiled, Yes
you do what you please first
then I can do what I please –

Oh, oh, oh! she cried
as the ambulance men lifted
her to the stretcher –
Is this what you call

making me comfortable?
By now her mind was clear –
Oh you think you're smart
you young people,

she said, but I'll tell you
you don't know anything.
Then we started.
On the way

we passed a long row
of elms. She looked at them
awhile out of
the ambulance window and said,

What are all those
fuzzy-looking things out there?
Trees? Well, I'm tired
of them and rolled her head away.

The Poem

It's all in
the sound. A song.
Seldom a song. It should

be a song – made of
particulars, wasps,
a gentian – something
immediate, open

scissors, a lady's
eyes – waking
centrifugal, centripetal

The Storm

A perfect rainbow! a wide
arc low in the northern sky
spans the black lake

troubled by little waves
over which the sun
south of the city shines in

coldly from the bare hill
supine to the wind which
cannot waken anything

but drives the smoke from
a few lean chimneys streaming
violently southward

The Bare Tree

The bare cherry tree
higher than the roof
last year produced
abundant fruit. But how
speak of fruit confronted
by that skeleton?
Though live it may be
there is no fruit on it.
Therefore chop it down
and use the wood
against this biting cold.

Labrador

How clean these shallows
how firm these rocks stand
about which wash
the waters of the world

It is ice to this body
that unclothes its pallors
to thoughts
of an immeasurable sea,

unmarred, that as it lifts
encloses this
straining mind, these
limbs in a single gesture.

The Bitter World of Spring

On a wet pavement the white sky recedes
mottled black by the inverted
pillars of the red elms,
in perspective, that lift the tangled

net of their desires hard into
the falling rain. And brown smoke
is driven down, running like
water over the roof of the bridge-

keeper's cubicle. And, as usual,
the fight as to the nature of poetry
– Shall the philosophers capture it? –
is on. And, casting an eye

down into the water, there, announced
by the silence of a white
bush in flower, close
under the bridge, the shad ascend,

midway between the surface and the mud,
and you can see their bodies
red-finned in the dark
water headed, unrelenting, upstream.

The Manoeuvre

I saw the two starlings
coming in toward the wires.
But at the last,
just before alighting, they

turned in the air together
and landed backwards!
that's what got me – to
face into the wind's teeth.

Raindrops on a Briar

I, a writer, at one time hipped on
painting, did not consider
the effects, painting,
for that reason, static, on

the contrary the stillness of
the object – the flowers, the gloves –
freed them precisely by that
from a necessity merely to move

in space as if they had been –
not children! but the thinking male
or the charged and deliver-
ing female frantic with ecstasies;

served rather to present, for me,
a more pregnant motion: a
series of varying leaves
clinging still, let us say, to

the cat-briar after last night's
storm, its waterdrops
ranged upon the arching stems
irregularly as an accompaniment.

A Note

When the cataract dries up, my dear
all minds attend it.
There is nothing left. Neither sticks
nor stones can build it up again
nor old women with their rites of green twigs

Bending over the remains, a body
struck through the breast bone
with a sharp spear – they have borne him
to an ingle at the wood's edge
from which all maidenhood is shent

– though he roared
once the cataract is dried up and done.
What rites can do to keep alive
the memory of that flood they will do
then bury it, old women that they are,
secretly where all male flesh is buried.

Seafarer

The sea will wash in
but the rocks – jagged ribs
riding the cloth of foam
or a knob or pinnacles
      with gannets –
are the stubborn man.

He invites the storm, he
lives by it! instinct
with fears that are not fears
but prickles of ecstasy,
a secret liquor, a fire
that inflames his blood to
coldness so that the rocks
seem rather to leap
at the sea than the sea
to envelop them. They strain
forward to grasp ships
or even the sky itself that
bends down to be torn
upon them. To which he says,
It is I! I who am the rocks!
Without me nothing laughs.

The Polar Bear

his coat resembles the snow
deep snow
the male snow
which attacks and kills

silently as it falls muffling
the world
to sleep that
the interrupted quiet return

to lie down with us
its arms
about our necks
murderously a little while

Sonnet in Search of an Author

Nude bodies like peeled logs
sometimes give off a sweetest
odor, man and woman

under the trees in full excess
matching the cushion of

aromatic pine-drift fallen
threaded with trailing woodbine
a sonnet might be made of it

Might be made of it! odor of excess
odor of pine needles, odor of
peeled logs, odor of no odor
other than trailing woodbine that

has no odor, odor of a nude woman
sometimes, odor of a man.